WHO AM I?

Who am I?

Titles in the series

Graceful and Galloping (Horse)
Heavy and Hoofed (Cow)
Loud and Crowing (Rooster)
Pink and Curly-tailed (Pig)

I am heavy and hoofed, gentle and slow.
I eat grass and hay.

WHO AM I?

By Moira Butterfield
Illustrated by Wayne Ford

Thameside Press

Distributed in the United States by
Smart Apple Media
1980 Lookout Drive
North Mankato, MN 56003

Printed in Hong Kong

  Library of Congress Cataloging-in-Publication Data
Butterfield, Moira, 1961-
  Cow / by Moira Butterfield.
    p. cm. — (Who am I?)
  Summary: Illustrations and simple text describe the different
parts of a dairy cow and its daily life.
  ISBN 1-929298-89-7
  1. Holstein-Friesian cattle—Juvenile literature. 2. Dairy
cattle—Juvenile literature. 3. Cows—Juvenile literature.
[1. Cows. 2. Dairy cattle.] I. Title.

SF199.H75 B88 2000
636.2'34—dc21   00-022291

9 8 7 6 5 4 3 2 1

Editor: Stephanie Turnbull
Designer: Helen James
Illustrator: Wayne Ford / Wildlife Art Agency
Consultant: Jock Boyd

My hoofs are hard.
My tail is long.
I'm black and white,
big and strong.
I like to stand all day and chew.
Now and then I softly moo.

Who am I?

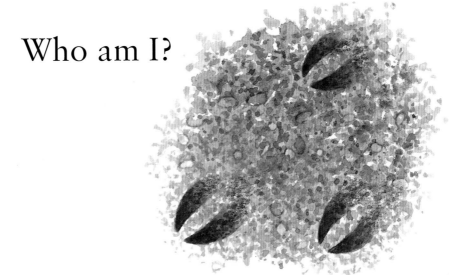

Here is my eye.

I live on a farm.
In summer I stand
in my field and
look around. What
animals can I see?

In hot weather
I stand under a
shady tree and doze.
What is in the tree
above my head?

Here is my mouth.

I love to eat grass.
I sit and chew each
mouthful for a long
time. This is called
chewing the cud.

Sometimes the farmer
gives me hay to eat.
When I am thirsty
I drink lots of water.

Here is my hoof.

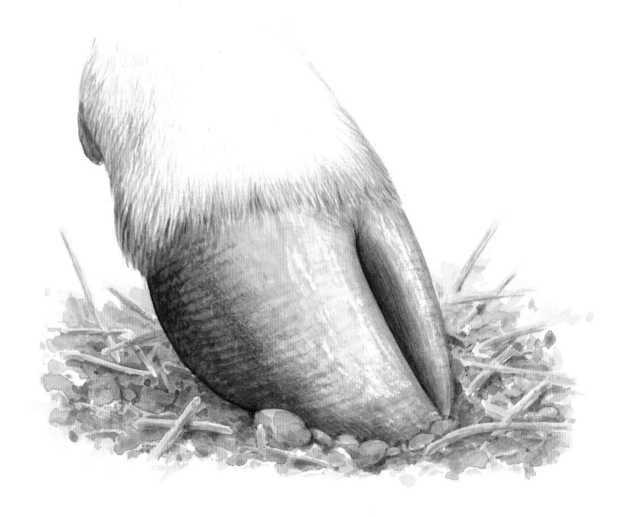

I have four hard hoofs.
They protect my feet
from sharp stones
and help me to walk
through muddy fields.

I am very heavy.
If I step on your toes
I will squash them.
I can kick hard,
so keep away from
my back legs.

Here is my skin.

It is thick and tough, but it feels soft because it is covered with lots of short hairs.

The hair on my skin is black and white. Some of my friends have brown or cream-colored hair.

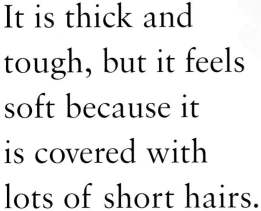

Here is my tail.

In summer flies
buzz around me
and annoy me.
I use my tail to
flick them away.

Be careful where
you walk in my
field because I make
lots of piles of
pooh. It is called
dung or manure.

Here is my udder.

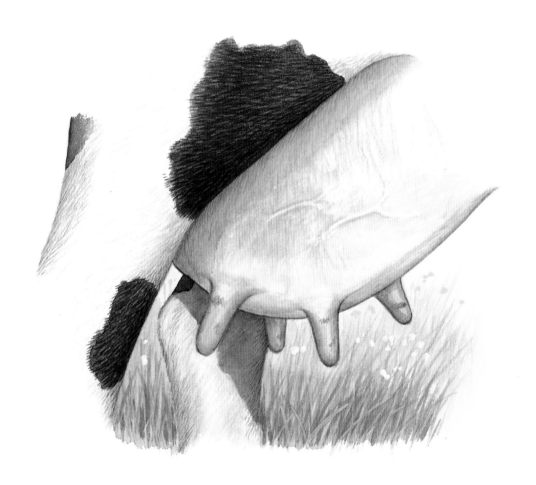

It fills with milk. Twice a day I go to the milking shed. The farmer milks me using a machine.

I don't mind being milked. It doesn't hurt, and the farmer gives me a tasty snack while I am there.

Here are my ears.

I twitch them when I hear a noise.
Then I tell my friends.

I open my mouth and...
moo!
Have you guessed who I am?

I am a cow.

I am called a
Holstein-Friesian.

Point to my...

hard hoofs

long tail

tough skin

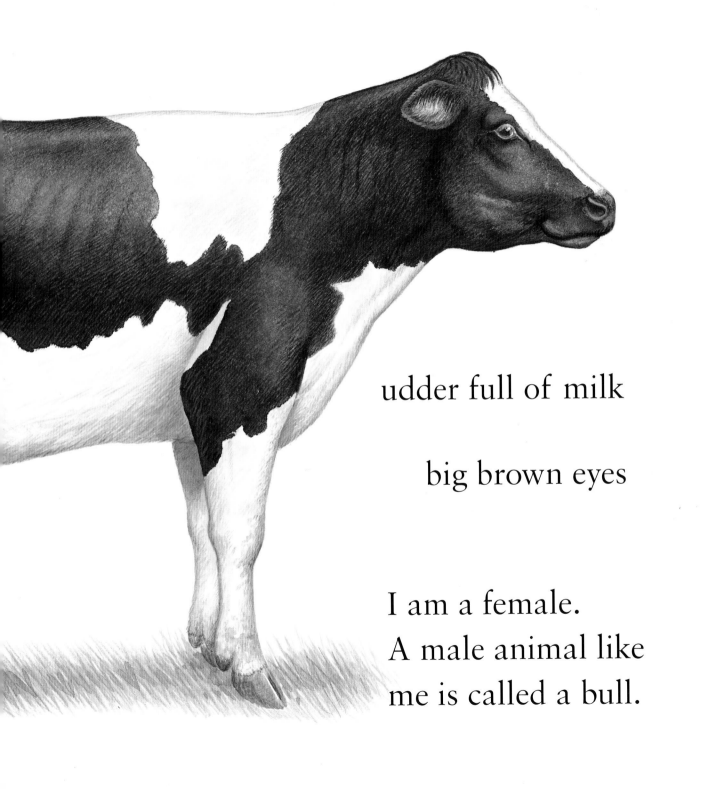

udder full of milk

big brown eyes

I am a female.
A male animal like
me is called a bull.

Here is my baby.

It is called a calf.
When it is small
it drinks my milk.
This helps it to grow
strong and healthy.

When it grows
bigger it eats grass
and hay. It runs
around the field
with other calves.

Here is my home.

I live with a group of cows called a herd.

How many cows can you see in the picture?
Can you spot the farm in the background?

Here are some other kinds of cows.

◄ This is a Jersey cow. Its milk is rich and creamy.

► Charolais cows are big and heavy with white or straw-colored hair.

Highland cows live in cold,
hilly places. They have thick,
shaggy hair to keep them warm.
Their horns are long and sharp.

Can you answer these questions about me?

Where do I live?

What do I like to eat?

Can you describe my skin?

Why are my hoofs useful?

What happens to me twice a day?

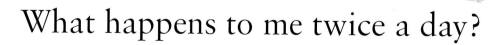

What is my baby called?

What sound do I make?

What annoys
me in summer?

What is the name
for a group of cows?

Can you name
some kinds of cows?

Here are some words to learn about me.

bull The name for a male animal like me.

calf The name for a baby cow or bull.

cud Grass that I chew for a long time. This helps me to swallow it easily.

dung The name for the piles of pooh I make. Another name for dung is manure.

hay Dried grass. The farmer sometimes gives me hay to eat.

herd A group of cows and bulls.

hoof My hard foot.

moo The deep, long sound that I make. Can you moo like me?

udder A bag of skin that hangs down under my tummy. It fills with milk every day.